PLAINS INDIANS

FIONA MACDONALD

INSIGHTS

PLAINS INDIANS

FIONA MACDONALD

BARRON'S

A QUARTO BOOK

First edition for the United States and Canada published
1993 by Barron's Educational Series, Inc.

Copyright © 1992 Quarto Publishing plc

All inquiries should be addressed to:
Barron's Educational Series, Inc.
250 Wireless Boulevard
Hauppauge, New York 11788

Library of Congress Catalog Card No. 93-16421

International Standard Book No. 0-8120-6376-7

Library of Congress Cataloging-in-Publication Data
Macdonald, Fiona.
  Plains Indians / Fiona Macdonald. — 1st ed. for the U.S. and Canada.
    p.   cm. — (Insights)
  Includes index.
  Summary: Explains the origins, societies, culture, and destruction of the
Plains Indians.
  ISBN 0-8120-6376-7
  1. Indians of North America—Great Plains—Juvenile literature.
[1. Indians of North America—Great Plains]   I. Title.   II. Series: Insights
(Barron's Educational Series, Inc.)
E78.G73M32   1993
978'.00497—dc20   93-16421
                                                                  CIP
                                                                   AC

This book was designed and produced by
Quarto Publishing plc
The Old Brewery, 6 Blundell Street, London N7 9BH

Consultant Dr. Karen Harvey

Art Director Nick Buzzard

Senior Editor Kate Scarborough
Copy Editor Scott Steedman
Designer Steve Wilson
Illustrators Sharon Smith, Sally Townsend
Picture Researcher Norman Bancroft Hunt

The Publishers would like to thank the following for their help in the
preparation of this book: Karen Ball, Jane Parker, and Ian West at
Museum of Plains Indians, Forge Cottage, Horsted Keynes, West Sussex.

Picture Acknowledgments
Quarto Publishing would like to thank the following for supplying pictures for this book:
photographed by Norman Bancroft Hunt, pages 10cl, 15al, 15cr, 17cl, 27ar, 27bl, 36cr,
41ar, 41cr, 42cr, 47cl, 49cr, 51cl, 51cr; Karl Bodmer, Atlas, photographed by
Norman Bancroft Hunt, pages 12br, 13bl, 26br, 31al, 33ar, 39ar, 42bl, 46l;
Will Channing, pages 27ar, 28bl, 43al; Mike Johnson, page 25br; Museum of the Great Plains,
page 49bl; Smithsonian Institution, National Archives, pages 10ar, 17bc, 20br, 21bl, 21b, 21br,
24cr, 23ar, 25al, 29ar, 30ar, 33br, 33bl, 37bl, 43br, 43bc, 43bl, 44b, 45br, 50ar, 50cl;
University of Oklahoma, pages 12bl, 30b; Ian West, pages 13ar, 18bc, 19al, 23br, 24bl, 26bl,
27ar, 34c, 37cr, 40br, 40al, 41bl, 42ar, 43ar, 47br, 47al, 47cl; Travel Photo International, page 14cr;
Key: a = above, b = below, l = left, r = right, c = center

While every effort has been made to trace and acknowledge all copyright
holders, we would like to apologize should any omissions have been made.

Manufactured in Hong Kong by J. Film Process Singapore Pte Ltd
Printed in Singapore by Star Standard Industries (Pte) Ltd

3456   9620   987654321

CONTENTS

WHO WERE THE PLAINS INDIANS?

"**W**hose voice first sounded on this land? The voice of the red people, who had only bows and arrows…" These proud words were spoken in 1865, by Mahpiua Luta (Red Cloud), one of the leaders of the Sioux people. He was protesting the destruction of the Native American way of life. By the end of the nineteenth century, Native Americans had been transformed from a free and independent group of peoples to outcasts in their own land.

▶ **Chief Powder Face**
One of the leaders of the Arapaho tribe. He carries a decorated lance (spear), which shows he is a member of a warrior society.

◀ **Strong, proud, and free**
This war bonnet was worn by a senior Blackfoot warrior. The man who wore this was believed to be strong, proud, and free.

This book looks at the life-style of one group of Native Americans, the Plains Indians, before this life-style was destroyed. Plains Indians is a modern term—Native Americans did not use it themselves. It refers to the people who once lived all over the Great Plains area of North America.

When European explorers arrived in America, in AD 1492, they found about two million Native Americans living there. These Indians (as the Europeans called them) belonged to at least 300 different tribes and spoke over 2,000 different languages. Famous Plains Indian tribes included the Cheyenne, the Blackfoot, and the Sioux. Each of these tribes spoke a different language. Their houses, clothes, and games were different, too. But

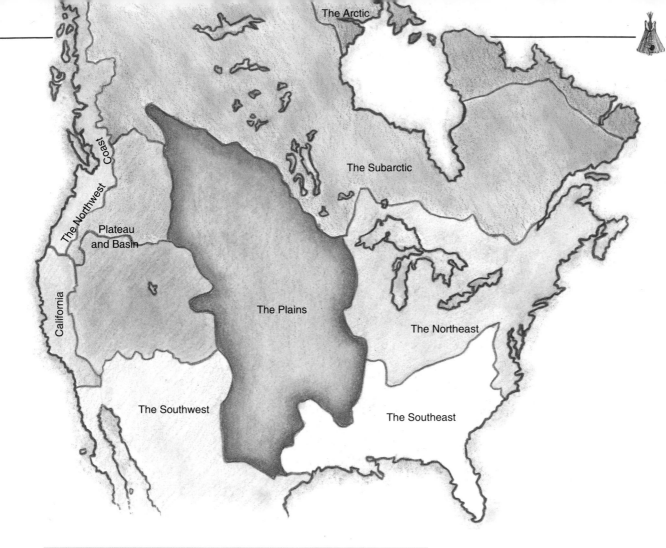

The Arctic

The Subarctic

The Northwest Coast

Plateau and Basin

California

The Plains

The Northeast

The Southwest

The Southeast

◀ **Homelands**

This map shows the homelands of the most powerful Native American peoples shaded orange-brown.

Over thirty different tribes of Native Americans lived in the Great Plains. Today, these peoples are often grouped together by historians and called Plains Indians. But in the past, Native American people called themselves by their ancient tribal names.

The Plains Indian homelands covered a vast area, including many different local environments. These ranged from the cold foothills of the Rockies in the northwest, to the hot lands of the Mississippi Valley in the south.

Some Plains Indian tribes were allies. Other tribes were enemies, and fought fiercely.

ASIA AND AMERICA

The Plains Indians—like all other native North Americans—are related to the peoples of northeastern Asia. The earliest settlers in North America arrived there from Siberia during the last Ice Age.

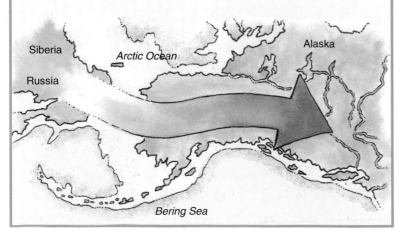

Siberia

Russia

Arctic Ocean

Alaska

Bering Sea

they all followed a way of life, based on hunting and farming, that made good use of the harsh local environment. They also shared religious beliefs.

Living on the Plains

Small groups of Native Americans had lived on the Great Plains for thousands of years. They grew corn, beans, and squash, and hunted wild animals and birds. They traveled everywhere on foot. They had no horses or wheeled transportation (Native American horses had died out in prehistoric times). Their traditional way of life was transformed by contact with European settlers, who arrived in America in huge numbers from the sixteenth century onward. Settlers brought horses, which

soon spread to the Plains. By about 1650, a new Plains Indians life-style started to develop. Sadly, it only lasted for about 300 years.

How do we know?

"Honest, hospitable, faithful, brave…" That is how George Catlin, one of the first white Americans to travel to the Great Plains, described the people he met there in 1832. But not everyone in nineteenth-century America shared his opinion. Sayings like "the only good Indian is a dead Indian" were widespread. Most white Americans thought Indians were bloodthirsty savages. They were not considered human beings by law, and were not even given American citizenship until 1924.

Because of this hostile image—which has continued until recently in Western films—it can be difficult to find out the truth about Plains Indians and their lives. But evidence of many different kinds has survived. There are clothes, weapons, pipes, musical instruments, paintings, carvings, and other beautiful objects made by Indians. There are paintings and drawings by late nineteenth- and early twentieth-century Indians, made to record their threatened way of life. None of the Indians kept written records. But many of their memories, traditions, and beliefs have been passed down by word of mouth to people living today.

Mato Tope

This painting of the warrior Mato Tope (Four Bears) was made during the 1830s by Karl Bodmer.

Mato Tope was famous for his bravery. Bodmer has shown him wearing a pair of buffalo horns. He was the only man in his tribe allowed to do this, a sign of great fame and honor.

Although Mato Tope was a great war leader, he did not wear the buffalo-horn headdress into battle. It was kept for special occasions, such as tribal ceremonies or meetings.

BUFFALO BILL

William F. Cody was a showman who toured America in the 1880s with a circus-style Wild West entertainment. His stage name was Buffalo Bill. The show featured Indian dances and the famous woman sharpshooter, Annie Oakley. Cody admired and was friendly with many Indians, including Chief Sitting Bull of the Sioux.

Cutting blocks of stone at the world's only pipestone quarry, now Pipestone National Monument, Minnesota. Indians liked to use the soft, pink stone found here for the bowls of the pipes they used in peacemaking ceremonies, and on other holy occasions.

THE GREAT PLAINS

As their name suggests, the Great Plains are vast. They stretch across central North America, covering more than 1.5 million square miles (4 million sq km). The land is flat or gently rolling with few trees. Today wheat and corn cover the Plains, but until this century, grass grew to the horizon in every direction. The climate can be blazing hot (100°F [38°C]) in summer and bitterly cold (–40°F [–40°C]) with heavy snow in winter.

The mighty Missouri River, the third longest in the world, crosses the Plains. It carries melted snow from the Rocky Mountains for over 2,700 miles (4,345 km) to the sea. The earliest Indian inhabitants of the Plains lived by the Missouri, to be sure of a steady supply of water for their crops. But there was always a danger of floods, when the great river overflowed its banks. One Indian tribe, the Mandan, told ancient legends about how they alone survived a great flood that covered the whole earth in swirling waters.

▼ **Mountain slopes**

Remote, high plains country. Rocks, loose stones, scrub bushes, and tough grass on low mountain slopes. In spite of their name, the Great Plains are not completely flat. In the west, toward the foothills of the high Rocky Mountains, the ground is rough and hilly. Rivers flow at the bottom of deep valleys, known as canyons.

GREAT PLAINS ENVIRONMENTS

There are many different environments within the Great Plains region, from steep mountain slopes to lush river valleys and dry, semidesert lands.

A SEA OF GRASS

Most of the Great Plains are grassland, often known as prairie land. (Prairie is the French word for meadow. The first French explorers to visit the Plains were reminded of green fields back home.)

Two different types of grasses grow on the Plains. To the west, where the land is drier, the grass is short and spiky. In the east, where there is more water, the grass grows tall.

Enemy evidence

Not all our evidence was produced by the Plains Indians themselves. There are nineteenth-century photos of Indian warriors and chiefs taken during talks with the American and Canadian governments. There are also tragic photos of Indian prisoners, or Indian families driven from their lands. Journalists wrote sensational newspaper reports on the white settlement of the Plains and on battles between Indians and settlers. Settlers also described the Indians in letters, and there are government reports dealing with Indian affairs.

Travelers' tales

Some of the best—though often romantic—descriptions of Plains Indian life come from nineteenth-century travelers. One of the earliest was written by two white Americans, Lewis and Clark who led the first scientific expedition to the Far West. Other travelers to the Plains painted the spectacular scenery—and the noble savages.

CLOTHES AND CUSTOMS

Another painting by Bodmer, of a woman from the Cree tribe, who lived in the northern Plains.

Bodmer's paintings were designed to carry a message about Native American culture to people back home in Europe. He wanted to portray the Indians as attractively as possible.

▼ A sacred place

As the explorer George Catlin clambered across this rough, rocky ground, in the spring of 1837, he was met by a group of fierce Indian warriors, standing guard. They refused to let him go any farther. "Go away—this is our sacred place," they said. "No white men may enter."

PIPES OF PEACE

Pipes were smoked by Indians to relax at home, or, more importantly, to welcome their friends, or make peace with their enemies. Tobacco, herbs, or willow bark were used. Many pipes, like these two, were beautifully made. The bowl of the top pipe is made from stone dug from the pipestone quarry.

▼ Making pipes

The pipe was chipped into shape using flint and obsidian, and hollowed out with flint drills. Finally, the pipe bowl was smoothed and polished, and fitted to a wooden or bone stem.

MORE THAN JUST GRASS

Not all prairie grassland was like the lush river meadows that French explorers had admired. In dry, rocky regions of the Great Plains, other plants, like this prickly cactus, grew alongside the grasses, making travel uncomfortable for people and animals. In wetter areas, progress could be halted by thickets of short, bushy trees, and the ground could be covered by a tangle of vines.

Buffalo herds

What attracted the Indians to this difficult environment? Put simply, the answer was food. The Plains were rich in wildlife, including bears, deer, foxes, wolves, and eagles. But most important were the great herds of buffalo, a strong, hairy animal like a large cow. One buffalo herd could contain up to a million animals. They wandered freely over the Plains, feeding on the short, tough grass, and moving north or south according to the season. The Indians hunted buffalo for more than

▼ Semidesert

In the Southwest, the Great Plains merge with the desert. Dry grass, cactus, and sage bushes grow here. The rainfall is less than 20 inches (500 mm) a year, compared to 40 inches (1000 mm) in the more fertile eastern plains. This means that the grass grows shorter, and dries out more quickly. But enough still grows to feed buffalo, elk, and deer.

MIGHTY RIVER

The Missouri flowed deep and fast. Its waters were colored dull yellow by mud. There were currents and whirlpools, and many floating trees, which had fallen into the river as the banks caved in. No wonder the Indians who lived alongside it treated it with respect, and early travelers reported that it was "the most frightful and discouraging prospect" for any explorer.

DESERTS, BUTTES, AND BLUFFS

In places, grassland was replaced by buttes (rocky outcrops) and bluffs (cliffs). In Wyoming and North and South Dakota, there were badlands, dry, stony slopes, where nothing grew. Few plants thrived in the far southwestern Plains. The land was dry, temperatures were hot, and prairie grass died.

▼ Traditional life-style

The Great Plains were not an easy place to live. Even though buffalo provided a plentiful supply of meat, crops were hard to grow and water was often scarce. For this reason, many early inhabitants settled close to rivers and streams.

Many Indians lived in villages, where they built solid, comfortable houses, surrounded by fields.

Villagers moved their homes to new sites every few years, when the soil in their fields became exhausted. As well as these village homes, Indians often spent part of the year camping in *tepees* (tents) as they traveled to hunt buffalo. Traditional Plains life-style was simple, but provided food, clothing, and shelter for the Indian people. Sadly, this traditional way of life was soon to change...

▼ Dangerous trade

The introduction of horses by settlers dramatically changed the lives of the Plains Indians, not only when traveling but also when hunting.

Some of the goods traded by the settlers were very useful. Trade blankets, made of thick, fleecy wool, helped to keep people warm in the bitter Plains winters. Glass beads were harmless, and attractive, too, although they eventually led to the disappearance of an ancient Indian skill. In the nineteenth century, they were used instead of traditional porcupine quill decorations on clothes and tepees.

Other traded goods were more dangerous. Guns helped the Plains people to hunt, but they were also used in battle. Whiskey, too, was a threat to the Indians' traditional way of life. Before the settlers arrived, alcohol was unknown so the Indian people had not learned of its dangers. Sadly, some Indian lives were destroyed by alcohol, but many more kept away from the white man's poison and tried to preserve their old way of life. Another result of contact between the Indians and settlers was the increase in illness. Settlers brought diseases that Indians had no resistance to, like smallpox.

its meat, making all sorts of essential goods from its skin, bones, fat, brains, even its bladder.

During the eighteenth century, European trappers and traders arrived in Plains Indian land. Some made the long journey on horseback from towns on the East Coast. Others sailed up the Missouri River, stopping at villages and setting up trading posts. These traders wanted furs and skins from foxes, buffalo, and beaver, to sell to customers back home. In return, they gave the villagers tobacco, beads, knives, whiskey, and guns.

Indians living in distant parts of the Plains also traveled to the villages to trade. They offered ermine tails and precious eagle feathers to the village Indians. In exchange, the villagers gave them corn, and, in later centuries, a share of the white traders' goods.

Foreign disease

Many Indians welcomed foreign trade. Guns, gunpowder, and iron blades for their weapons all made life easier. The traders' tobacco was better than their own, and both men and women admired the brightly colored glass beads they brought. But the whiskey was a disaster and European diseases, caught from infected traders, were even more damaging to the Native Americans. They has no natural resistance to these diseases, and no medicines to fight them with. Smallpox in particular led to hundreds of thousands of deaths.

▲ Traditional crafts

The Plains Indians decorated their clothes, houses, and jewelry with scenes showing everyday activities, festivals, and special occasions. Some of the designs were hundreds of years old. This disk of carved shell was made to decorate the neckline of a shirt, or to be worn as a pendant. It shows two hunters dancing. This design originated with peoples who lived in the Mississippi Valley about AD 1400, before many of the Plains Indian people came to settle there.

DOG POWER

Indians made sleds of tepee poles and buffalo skin to carry their belongings. It was called a *travois*, and was traditionally pulled by dogs. This nineteenth-century photograph shows a Cheyenne woman with her dog. He is pulling a travois covered with a decorated buffalo hide.

Sioux warriors were among the most famous Indian riders. They performed amazing acrobatics on horseback, to escape from enemy arrows, or to spear their prey.

HORSE CULTURE

Contact with white traders changed life for the Plains Indians in many ways. But the greatest change of all was the arrival of the horse. This happened gradually, from 1650 to 1800. At first, the Indians bought or stole horses from tribes living closer to the white settlers. Later, they caught untamed ponies from the herds that had escaped from the settlers' control. These beautiful mustangs now roam wild over large parts of the Great Plains.

▶ **Prized possessions**

The Indians valued their horses, and liked to provide them with fine harnesses. This bridle ornament was made by craftworkers of the Crow tribe, using deerskin and beads.

▼ **Sioux saddlebag**

Indian hunters and warriors traveled light. They carried basic food rations and spare ammunition in saddlebags like these. This bag is made from deerskin and decorated with beads, dyed horsehair, and cone-shaped pieces of tin.

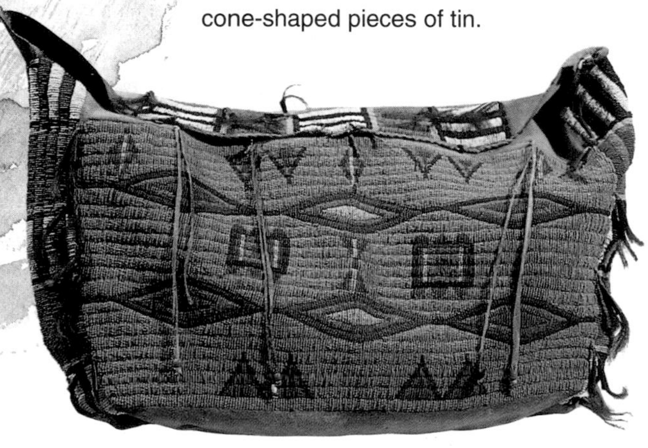

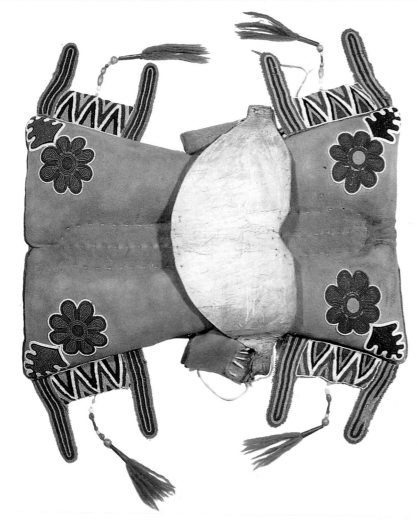

Indians admired horses and knew how useful they could be. Some tribes were so impressed by horses that they called them sacred dogs. The horse could pull four times more weight than the Indians' other helper, the dog. Horses were faster and more obedient, and most important, they could carry people.

A transportation revolution

The horse revolutionized Plains Indian life. Soon, Indians traded, captured, or stole horses wherever they could. A family's wealth was measured in the number of horses it owned. Tepees, the Indians' portable homes, were made bigger and more comfortable. Travel was quicker, so everyone had more free time. Most important of all, horses transformed hunting, raiding, and war.

Hunting

Other than a few kinds of deer, the horse was the fastest animal on the Great Plains. The Indians used the horse's speed to outrun their prey, and relied on its courage and intelligence when they went in for the kill. A horse was trained to chase and overtake a buffalo, keeping to the right-hand side so the rider could shoot at close range.

▲ Riding in style
This saddle was designed to be used with its own special blanket. The saddle is made of wood, and the blanket is made of thick cloth, padded to protect the horse's back. The blanket is decorated with appliqué—fabric and leather cutouts in bright colors sewn onto the blanket cloth.

PROUD SYMBOLS

Indian warriors painted their horses with designs that told everyone about their achievements in battle. Similar patterns were painted on warriors' shirts. Here are some of the best-known designs.

▲ This string of horse tracks records the number of raids the rider has been on.

▲ These lightning zigzag lines are painted on to encourage speed in the horse.

▲ These are the markings of one society—a group of warriors.

NATIONS AND CHIEFS

The ancestors of the Plains Indians first reached North America between 50,000 and 10,000 years ago. They walked across from the northeastern tip of Asia (now part of Russia) to the northwestern tip of America (now the state of Alaska). At that time, the two continents were connected by a land bridge, a strip of dry land that disappeared under the sea at the end of the last Ice Age. This huge migration continued for many centuries.

America is an enormous land, and the first migrants were few. The new inhabitants lived in isolated groups, which they thought of as separate nations or tribes. Each tribe developed its own language and its own way of life. The tribes were proud of their separate identities, which

► Plains Indians' territories

1 Sarcee
2 Plains Cree
3 Blackfoot
4 Gros Ventre
5 Assiniboin
6 Plains Ojibwa
7 Crow
8 Teton Sioux
9 Hidatsa
10 Mandan
11 Arikara
12 Yanktonai Sioux
13 Santee Sioux
14 Cheyenne
15 Ponca
16 Omaha
17 Yankton Sioux
18 Iowa
19 Oto
20 Pawnee
21 Arapaho
22 Kansa
23 Missouria
24 Kiowa
25 Kiowa-Apache
26 Osage
27 Comanche
28 Wichita
29 Quapaw
30 Lipan Apache
31 Tonkawa
32 Sauk and Fox

INDIAN SOCIETY

Indian men and women owed loyalty to several different groups. First was their band, or family group. Band members depended on one another for survival.

Clan loyalties were also important. Marriages might be arranged between distant relations belonging to the same clan.

Loyalty to a tribe was especially important in wartime. Tribal chiefs were politicians and battle leaders. The bravest and wisest men, chosen from all the bands and clans that made up the tribe, acted as their deputies.

FAMOUS CHIEFS

Many Indian chiefs were wise leaders. The best known lived at the time the Indian people were coming into contact with white settlers and American soldiers. They were recorded in paintings, photographs, and government reports, as well as in Indian songs and legends. Many of these leaders tried bravely to preserve the Indian way of life.

▲ Standing Bear, chief of the Poncas. He fought a major lawsuit to protect Indians' civil rights.

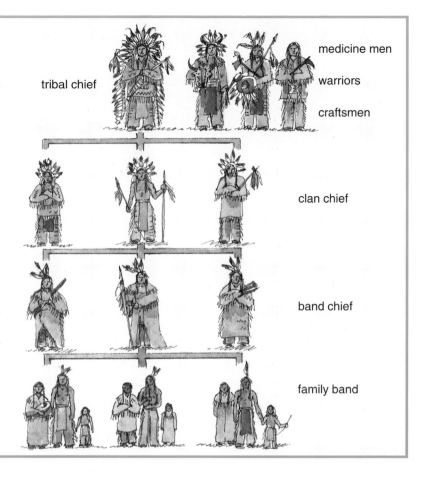

tribal chief

medicine men

warriors

craftsmen

clan chief

band chief

family band

were reflected in their names. For example, the Sioux called themselves "Dakota," which simply meant "people" in their own language.

Sometimes these tribes traded together peacefully. At other times, they became caught up in bitter, bloody wars. Strong tribes, like the Blackfoot, Sioux, and Comanche, attacked smaller, weaker tribes, such as the Mandan and Hidatsa. They wanted to control and take advantage of the best hunting grounds.

Chiefs and families

Indian tribes were usually led by a chief. He was chosen by the people for his strength, bravery, and wisdom. Sometimes sons followed their fathers as chiefs, but first they had to prove that they were fearless and wise. Chiefs ruled with the help of experienced warriors and other respected members of the tribe. Men skilled in healing—medicine men—also gave advice.

▲ Sitting Bull, leader of the Sioux. He fought and argued bravely to defend his people.

▲ Keokuk, chief of the Sauk tribe. A photograph taken when he was old. When young, he resisted the settlers.

▲ Dull Knife, a famous Cheyenne war leader. He was the last chief to fight against U.S. troops.

▲ Gall, chief of the Sioux. He fought against U.S. General George Custer, enemy of the Indians.

FAMILY LIFE

Indian tribes were divided into bands, or smaller groups. There might be twenty families—a hundred or so people—in one band. The band members were often related, as cousins, uncles, or aunts. They traveled, worked, fought together, and shared food.

It was usual for a girl to marry between twelve and fourteen. Men might be a little older—unless they were rich, they would need to prove their strength and bravery first, to attract a bride. Some couples married for love. But often marriages between families were arranged by the parents. New husbands were expected to give presents—like a horse, blankets, or buffalo skins—to their bride's father. Rich men had several wives, but women were not allowed to have more than one husband.

Small families

Most Plains Indian families were quite small. Each mother might have two or three children. Indian life was hard, and babies who were sick or handicapped often did not survive long.

Within the family, men and women had different jobs to do. They were all essential for survival.

The Plains Indians lived close to the natural world,

Men's work

Within the family, men and women had different jobs to do. Boys and girls were trained for their adult tasks from an early age. Men fought and hunted, and went on raids.

▼ Women's work

Women did not fight, and rarely went hunting. One woman is reported to have gone on a dangerous raid, but she was exceptional. She explained her behavior by saying she was so much in love with her husband that she wanted to die fighting alongside him. More usually, women cooked, cleaned, cared for children and sick people, dug in the fields, and grew crops.

CLOTHING AND SHELTER

Women prepared the hides of buffalo skins used to make clothing and tepees. First the skin was pegged to the ground (below) or pulled on a frame (above). Then it was scraped clean of fat and hair using a bone scraper (right).

Although women worked hard, they did not play much part in public life. Only men joined in most religious ceremonies; women and children stood by and watched, or sometimes sang. The men drew strength from the women's emotional support:

Look at that young man
He is feeling good
Because his sweetheart
Is watching him.

and their lives changed with the seasons. In the spring, they planted crops and caught young birds and animals. In the summer, they harvested corn, and gathered all kinds of wild fruits. There were extra buffalo hunts in the autumn, to stock up on food. In the winter, when snow covered the windswept Plains, everyone concentrated on trying to survive.

All these seasons were marked by special ceremonies. These were held to celebrate harvests and hunts, but they had another purpose, too. They encouraged the "good order" of sun and rain, birth and rebirth, to continue forever. At some ceremonies, like the Sun Dance, men endured painful ordeals. They offered their suffering to the gods, and asked them to keep on providing for the

NAMED BY THE SPIRIT

In some tribes, children—especially boys—were not named at birth. Instead, when they were about twelve, they went to a quiet lonely place, and asked the Great Spirit for guidance. They hoped to receive a vision of an animal or bird. For the rest of their life, that would be their own special creature, and they took its name.

KIOWA DAUGHTERS

Two young girls from the Kiowa tribe, dressed in their best clothes. Their long deerskin shirts are elaborately decorated with (right) elk teeth and (left) bead embroidery. Fine clothes like this were only worn by children from wealthy familes. Children were taught to be proud of their hair. They combed and oiled it to keep it smooth and glossy.

▶ **A child's toy**
This doll, given to a young Sioux girl to play with, is more than 100 years old. It is made out of materials that were readily available on the Great Plains at that time—buffalo skin and glass and metal beads, purchased from white traders. Its clothing shows Sioux women's costume in a simple form—a long overshirt and leggings, both made of skins.

world and its people. Ceremonies were also held to mark important stages in a person's life, from birth through adolescence to death and burial.

Fun and games

Other seasonal festivals were less serious and more like holidays. At various times of the year, Plains Indians made time for sports and games. They skated and played shinny (ice hockey) during the winter, and raced, played lacrosse, and a game with hoops and spears in the summer. They also held shooting competitions and gambled in a game that involved throwing seeds and stones marked somewhat like dice. By the eighteenth century, the Indians played ball game just for fun.

When times were hard, the Plains Indians relied on their family band. Indian men also belonged to ritual societies, with names like "the Bulls" or "the Stone Hammers." Members of these societies promised to help one another at all times. They also acted like policemen in the camp, and arranged hunting or raiding parties. They took part in dances, wearing magnificient skins and masks.

▲ Indian fashion

This wealthy young woman from the Dakota people is dressed in Indian clothes influenced by European fashions. Instead of a skin overshirt, she wears a long cloth robe, trimmed with bones, ribbons, beads, and coins. She also wears embroidered moccasin boots. Her hair is plaited, in reservation style. This suggests that her people were moved from their homeland by the U.S. government and settled in camps, known as reservations.

FAMILY BURIAL

In many tribes, dead people were placed on wooden platforms until their flesh rotted away. Then their bones were buried. As one Sioux explained, "All my relatives are lying here in the ground, and when I fall to pieces, I am going to fall to pieces here."

IN HARMONY WITH NATURE

Plains Indians worshiped the Great Spirit, who had created them, and all the other living things on the earth. Indian men and women tried to live in harmony with nature, taking care not to damage the unique environment of the Great Plains. They relied on nature's resources to keep them alive. They believed that success and failure in hunting or farming were sent by the Great Spirit. If people "trod carefully on the earth" they could expect a generous reward.

The Indians kept a sharp eye on the animals, birds, and weather of the Plains. They feared the deep, swirling waters of rivers during a flood, believing that the waves and currents were evil spirits. Many Indian groups would not eat fish, for fear of offending these invisible powers. Unlike white American hunters, Indians only killed animals for food. They believed that killing for sport or pleasure was more than wasteful—it was also an insult to the Great Spirit. They dreaded thunderstorms, which flattened their crops. To

MEDICINE BAG

A modern copy of a traditional medicine bag, made in the shape of a turtle. Indians believed that magic bags like these kept their owners safe from harm, or brought good luck. This medicine bag contained an umbilical cord, preserved at birth, and designed to be hung on a baby's cradle.

▼ **Dog dancer**
A Hidatsa chief, taking part in the Dog Dance. Painted by Karl Bodmer, 1834. After sacrificing two dogs, warriors danced around, taking bites from the meat as it cooked. Only men who had killed an enemy in battle could dance.

SUN DANCE

Many tribes performed versions of this dance. Taking part could mean different things to different people, but the dance was always an offering to the Great Spirit, designed to bring safety and prosperity to the tribe. Only men took part. The dancers leaped or crawled in a huge circle around a tall pole, copying the way the sun moves in the sky. By doing this, they encouraged the sun to send light and warmth.

In many tribes, the Sun Dance also involved suffering. Men fixed ropes to their skin, and danced until the skin ripped and they could break free. They did this to give thanks to the Great Spirit or to ask for a favor.

◀ Painted buffalo skull, worn in the Sun Dance.

MAGIC TREASURES

Objects like these were used in ceremonies designed to bring Indian people closer to the Great Spirit.
Top: a Cree dance hoop, carried and shaken during the Sun Dance. Made of wood, cloth, sinews, and hawk feathers.

Center: a drumstick, made out of painted wood, with a stone head padded with deerskin.
Bottom: a Crow drum cover, used by dancers or by the musicians who played for them. It is decorated with cosmic symbols—sun and moon.

explain violent downpours, medicine men told ancient legends about the Thunderbird, which shot deadly arrows of lightning from its clawed feet.

Leisure time

Before the Europeans came, the Plains Indians had spent most of their days hunting or traveling in search of food. But with horses to help them, they had more free time. They used this for dances and other religious ceremonies, for telling and listening to stories and legends, or simply for pleasant conversation. As one traveler reported, "They are fond of fun and good cheer, and can laugh easily."

THE TRAVELING LIFE

Tribes like the Sioux and the Blackfoot were nomads who never lived in permanent villages. They made tepee camps which could be packed up and moved at very short notice, to follow the wandering buffalo herds. Nomads moved camp six to eight times every year. When they wanted corn or beans, they traded furs with Indians living in villages. Other tribes, like the Pawnee, were seminomads, following the buffalo in the summer but returning to village homes for the cold winter months.

Once horses came to the Plains, many more Indian tribes, including the powerful Cheyenne and Crow tribes, decided to live as nomads. With horses, they could travel much faster and farther across the Plains. They could move their whole families and set up camp in the best hunting grounds.

But even with horses, traveling through the thick prairie grass was hard work. In the river valleys to the south, the grass could grow shoulder-high.

EASY TO CARRY

This wooden bowl was used by Sioux nomads, traveling in the East Dakota region of the Plains. Wood was fairly light and also unbreakable. This made it a sensible choice to carry on long journeys.

In 1724, one Pawnee leader lamented that "our wives and children die under the burden" of long, difficult journeys. Early white travelers reported that they could not keep up with their Indian guides, until the guides showed them the best way to walk—with their toes turned in.

Winter camp

Snow lay thick on the ground in the winter, and nomads could not travel. So they pitched their tepees in sheltered valleys. If they could, they made camp in the woods, because the trees protected them from the icy wind. Men went hunting on foot, wearing snowshoes. Women gathered firewood, and the horses pawed the ground to uncover grass beneath the snow. It was an anxious time—food

CARTS WITHOUT WHEELS

Blackfoot women riding and leading horses, each pulling a travois heavily laden with household goods. Typical household equipment included clothes; rugs and blankets; spoons, cups, and bowls made of wood and horn; at least one fireproof cooking pot; baskets and leather pouches containing grain and dried food; knives, medicines, and tobacco.

▼ Slow progress
Even with horses to help, nomad journeys could take a long time. The whole group could not travel much faster than its slowest member. If dogs were still used, this meant an average speed of only 5 or 6 miles (8–10 km) per day. Old and sick people, who could not keep up with the rest, were sometimes left behind to die. No one liked doing this, but it was necessary if the tribe was to survive.

As well as traveling faster, horses made journeys easier in other, surprising ways. They were more obedient than dogs—loads were lost and bundles overturned when dogs forgot their duties and chased after a rabbit!

◀ Keeping watch
Warriors on lookout duty at the back of a nomad convoy. Usually, women and children traveled at the front of the convoy, so the men could ride behind, guarding them from surprise attack. Not every warrior could afford enough horses for his whole family to ride. Women and children took turns walking beside their family's horse.

▶ Disappearing village
Nomad peoples had to be ready to pack up camp at very short notice, if their scouts sent news of a wandering buffalo herd, or of enemies on the prowl nearby. An entire tepee village could be taken down in less than five hours. Only a few traces remained, to show that a whole band had once lived there…

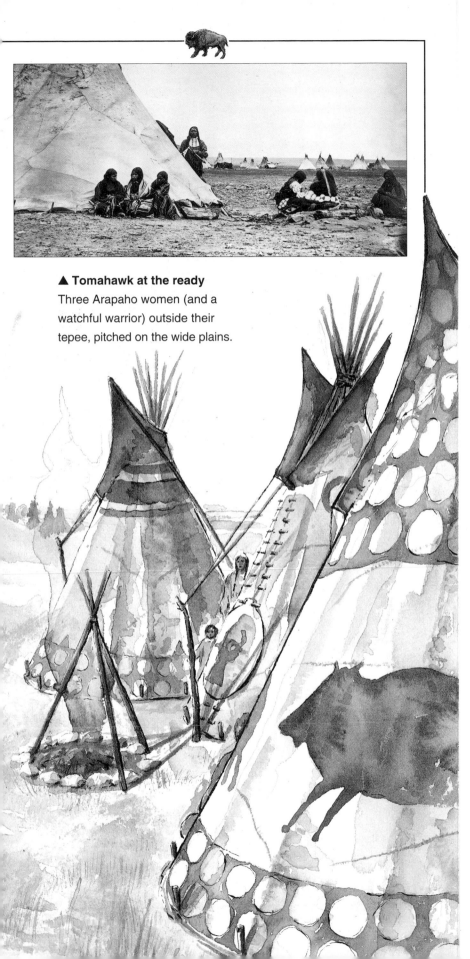

▲ Tomahawk at the ready
Three Arapaho women (and a watchful warrior) outside their tepee, pitched on the wide plains.

might run short, or tepees might be buried in a blizzard. No wonder Plains Indians prayed, "May I live to see the spring."

Following the buffalo

Plains Indians lived alongside buffalo from the cradle to the grave. Young babies were kept warm with blankets of buffalo fur, and corpses (dead bodies) were wrapped in a buffalo skin cloak, to shelter their spirits in the world of the dead. The buffalo provided almost everything the Indians needed. As well as meat and blood (which was drunk fresh), the buffalo gave fat, bones, hides, and hair.

Rawhide—untreated buffalo skin—was used to make ropes and wallets (called *parfleches*). Treated hides were used for tepee covers, or were sewn with thread made from buffalo sinews to make clothes and shoes. The skins were greased and softened with buffalo fat and brains. The thickest sinews were made into bowstrings. Containers for gunpowder and spoons for cooking could be

▼ Stampede
A herd of buffalo charging—or stampeding—toward a (rather brave) cameraman. This photograph was taken in Oklahoma, in the south of the Great Plains region. Once a herd had started to stampede like this, it could be driven by shouts or gunshots toward the place where they could be slaughtered.

▲ Under cover
Plains Indian hunters, disguised in white wolf skins, creeping close to a herd of buffalo. This picture was painted by George Catlin in 1831–32. The hunters had to approach the buffalo downwind, otherwise their human scent—and the smell of the wolf skins—would be carried toward the buffalo, and frighten them away.

A HUNDRED USES

Nobody knows exactly
how many different uses
the Plains Indians found
for different parts of
slaughtered buffalo, but
there were probably at
least a hundred. As well
as food, clothes, and
tepees, buffalo carcasses
provided sinews for bow
strings and sewing thread;
bones for ice skates,
shovels, war clubs, and
dice; stomachs and
bladders to make
containers; tails to make
fly swatters and whips;
hair to make headdresses
or to stuff saddles and
pillows; and hoofs to be
boiled to make glue.

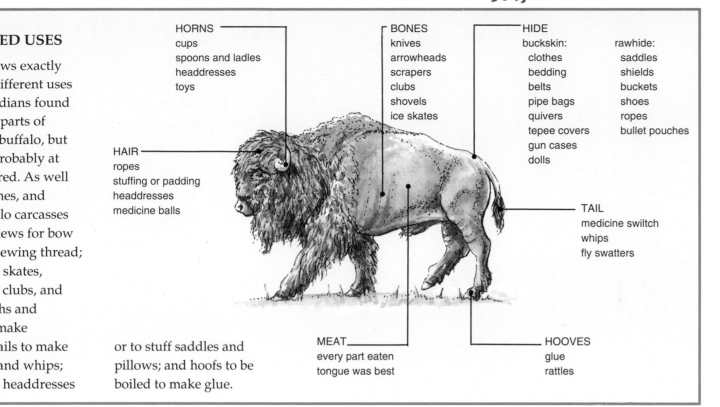

HORNS
cups
spoons and ladles
headdresses
toys

HAIR
ropes
stuffing or padding
headdresses
medicine balls

BONES
knives
arrowheads
scrapers
clubs
shovels
ice skates

HIDE
buckskin:
  clothes
  bedding
  belts
  pipe bags
  quivers
  tepee covers
  gun cases
  dolls

rawhide:
  saddles
  shields
  buckets
  shoes
  ropes
  bullet pouches

TAIL
medicine switch
whips
fly swatters

MEAT
every part eaten
tongue was best

HOOVES
glue
rattles

▼ **Hunting skills**
The normal way for Plains
Indians to hunt buffalo after the
introduction of horses was to
chase them. They fired arrows,
often at full gallop, to kill them.

carved from buffalo horn, and hair was used
to pad saddles, or plaited to make strong,
lightweight bridles and halters for the Indians'
horses. Stomachs and bladders were turned into
buckets; bones were carved to form tools,
whistles, and skates for the winter.

Hunting on foot

Traditionally, Indians hunted buffalo on foot.
Disguised as animals, they crept close to the herd,
aiming to kill at least one animal before the others
took fright. At other times, they stampeded the
animals into buffalo jumps, where the panic-
stricken beasts became trapped in narrow valleys
or fell over cliffs. All able-bodied men and women
took part in hunts like these. Dead animals were
butchered on the spot. Then women, children,
and dogs carried the precious meat home.

▼ Elegance and ease

Catlin was impressed by the Sioux way of life, as they sheltered in their tepees, waiting to trade with the white settlers. He reported "there was an abundance of food to eat," and that all the Sioux people he met were honest, peaceful, well dressed, and well fed. The Sioux men were resting after a successful hunting season, and enjoying "pleasures and amusements, idleness and ease, with no business hours to attend to, no taxes, no rents, no beggars…"

Tepee life was not always this easy, of course. But Catlin was convinced that it could be just as pleasant and civilized, in its own way, as village life anywhere else in the world.

HOUSES AND HOMES

The Plains Indians built houses to suit their life-styles, using whatever materials they could find. Very few trees grew on the Plains, and there was not much building stone. So nomads made tepees from buffalo skins, while villagers settled in lodges built mainly of earth.

Indian buildings were made with great skill. Their builders took great care to make them strong, weatherproof, and attractive. An average-sized tepee was made out of 20 or 30 pinewood poles, cut from young tree trunks about 25 feet (almost 8 m)

RICH AND POOR

Some Indians were rich, others were poor. Wealth was measured in possessions. These differences in wealth could also be seen in Indian houses. The grass lodge (right) looks dark and drafty. The bark tepee (far right) looks damp and cold. In contrast, some earth lodges, like those in the Mandan village (top right), were warm and dry, and well furnished with rugs, skins, and curtained beds.

◄ Camp life

The camp illustrated here is Cheyenne. Tepee camps could be very large. In 1831 George Catlin visited a camp containing over 600 tepees, where a tribe of Dakota Sioux were living. Both the Cheyenne and the Sioux were powerful northern nations. Their life-styles would have been fairly similar. What was it like?

tall. Tepee skins were cleaned and bleached before being painted with patterns in bright colors and decorated with porcupine quills. Each tepee housed one family.

Plains lodges

Earth lodges were larger and more solid than tepees. A wealthy family might build one 50 feet (about 15 m) across. Lodges were usually circular, and built over a shallow hole in the ground. The walls were made of a timber frame covered in hard-packed earth. They were usually about six and a half feet (2 m) high. The thick walls kept out the winter cold and held up a domed timber roof. This was thatched with rough brushwood and topped with another thick layer of earth. The whole house was coated with a layer of clay which baked hard in the summer sun, keeping the water out year-round.

▲ **Village homes**
A Mandan earth-lodge village, built on low cliffs on the banks of the Mississippi. The Mandan people preferred a raised site, to protect their homes from floods. A painting by Catlin, around 1831. At the front of the picture you can see *bull-boats* made of thin poles covered with buffalo hide.

▲ Grass lodge, made by the Wichita tribe who lived a nomadic life during the summer months, hunting on the southern Plains. Thick bunches of dried grass are fixed to curved wooden poles.

▲ A bark tepee, made by the Sauk and Fox tribe from the northern Plains. Strips of bark, stretched over a wooden frame, are held in place by twigs. This tepee dates from 1881. Nine people lived here.

HUNTING AND GATHERING

Buffalo were incredibly useful. But Plains Indians could not survive on buffalo meat alone. They also relied on wild fruits, berries, and other foods gatherd from the Plains, and used furs, feathers, and bones from other wild animals to decorate their clothes, tepees, and weapons.

Gathering was woman's work. As soon as they were old enough to be useful, children helped too. Many different kinds of berries were picked from short, scrubby bushes growing among the thick Great Plains grass. Delicacies included tiny strawberries and fruits like juicy wild plums. Some of these fruits were eaten fresh, but most were carefully sorted and spread out in the sun to dry. The dried fruits would provide vitamins and

▼ Essential kit
Every hunting man would have a knife or dagger. Early daggers were made of stone or bone; later ones of metal imported from early settlers. They were also used for fighting.

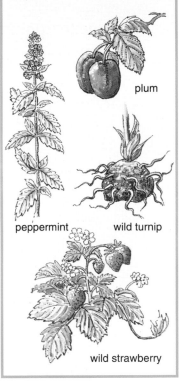
OTHER PREY

The buffalo was not the only wild animal hunted by Plains Indians. Here are seven examples of other wild animals caught by Indians. Each was prized for different reasons. In some areas even wolves and bears were killed and their skins used for decoration.

▲ The porcupine was caught for its quills which were used for weaving.

▲ The beaver was considered sacred and its skins used to make healing medicine bundles.

▲ The tail feathers of these bald eagles were used for achievement marks.

sweetness through the cold winter months. Herbs, including peppermint, were also picked and dried. They were then mixed with pounded meat, to keep it fresh in the stores.

In the river valleys, women picked rushes to weave baskets and mats. They also peeled willow twigs and dried the bark to make a harsh-tasting substitute for tobacco. They collected shells to make jewelry, and used digging sticks made of buffalo bone to uproot wild turnip which grew all over the Plains.

Prized animal

Men killed more than buffalo. They also went hunting eagles, owls, hawks, foxes, beavers, deer, porcupines, and ermine. Then they used the feathers and skins from these beautiful creatures to decorate their clothes. Eagle feathers were rare and very valuable. In many tribes, only the bravest warriors were allowed to wear them. Bones from the elk (a large kind of deer) were highly prized, and young men made whistles from them. They played tunes, copying the sounds elks make during the mating season. After dark, they sent secret messages to their girlfriends in musical code.

DEATH TRAP

Plains Indians hunted birds and animals by using decoy traps. The hunter dug a pit big enough to hide inside, and covered the surface with twigs, leaves, and dried grass. He made peepholes to spy through.

Then he placed his decoy animal—often a stuffed wolf—at one edge of the pit, and waited for hungry birds and animals to investigate. As they came close to the decoy, the hunter speared them, or tried to catch them with his bare hands.

▲ The elk was admired for its bravery. Its horns and bones were used as tools or musical instruments.

▲ Plains tribes watched owls to learn about night wisdom and gentle ways. They used its feathers.

▲ The ermine was highly prized for its fine pelt or skin. It was used as trimmings on clothes.

▲ Indians caught the pronghorn antelope by running it into exhaustion.

FOOD

▼ **Colored corn**

Maize (sweet corn) was the Plains Indians' most important crop. It was native to South America, and grew well on the eastern Plains. Each color tasted different.

In good years, the Plains Indians ate well. After a buffalo kill, an adult might eat as much as four pounds (almost 2 kg) of meat a day. Indians ate thin slices of raw meat from the buffalo's hump, or feasted on the perishable parts—the liver, brains, blood, and kidneys. These soft foods were easy for young children and toothless people to suck and swallow. Puddings were made from ground turnips, or berries mixed with fresh blood.

Indians who grew crops feasted at harvest time. They held a green (fresh) corn feast when their maize was ripe. Boiled corn was ladled out into wooden bowls and everyone ate their fill. Villagers also enjoyed meals of pumpkins, beans, and squash.

Shortages and sharing

More than anything else, the Indians feared starvation. Nomads knew that the buffalo moved in unpredictable ways. Herds might disappear for months on end, leaving hunters to search

BASIC TOOLS

Women used digging sticks and shovels made from wood or buffalo bone. Containers for carrying water to young seedlings were made from wood, pottery, buffalo hide, or buffalo stomachs. Before settlers arrived, knives and sickles for cutting corn were made from sharp-edged flints. Later, they were made of metal.

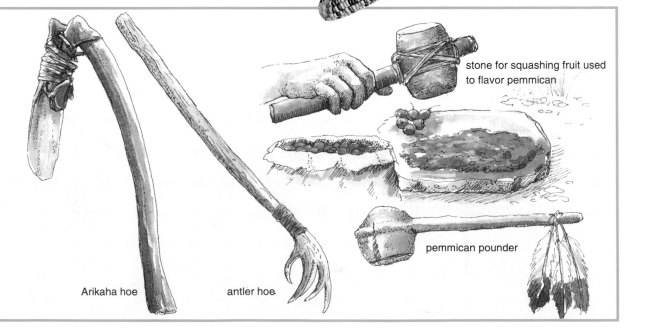

stone for squashing fruit used to flavor pemmican

pemmican pounder

Arikaha hoe

antler hoe

desperately for rabbits and deer to feed their families. Villagers had other problems. They knew that rains could fail, leaving them to watch their crops shrivel in the summer sun.

The Plains Indians coped with these dangers by sharing generously with people in need. They never knew when it might be their family's turn to go hungry. Most Indian households kept a pot of stew cooking gently over the fire all day long. Anyone who needed food could help themselves. People who abused this hospitality were scorned.

Storing food

Indians also made careful arrangements for storing food, so they would not go hungry when game was scarce. The best quality buffalo meat was cut into thin strips and hung up to dry. Tougher cuts were made into uncooked sausages, or mixed with herbs, berries, and marrow fat (from inside bones) and packed into a solid block. Grain was stored in pits lined with dried grass. Beans were dried in the sun and then kept in woven baskets.

INDIAN MEALS

Indian chiefs were generous hosts. Proudly, they invited visitors to share their meals. To honor their guests, they did not eat with them. Instead, visitors were served first, with food cooked by the chief's wives. The chief helped the guest to the tastiest morsels, and than sat waiting. He would not eat until his guest had finished.

At family meals, the men ate first. Women and girls ate later.

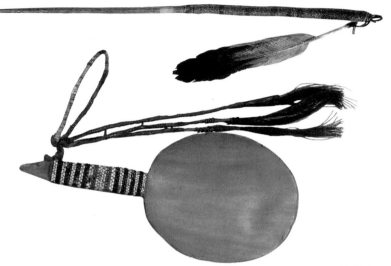

▲ Well designed
These cooking tools are simple, but well designed and beautifully made. The meat skewer (above) is made of wood, decorated with beads and feathers. The spoon (below) is made of polished buffalo horn, with a finely carved handle. The skewer was made by the Crow tribe; the spoon by Sioux craftworkers.

◄ Home and dry
Racks of buffalo meat, drying in the strong Plains sunshine. After drying like this, the meat would last throughout the winter months.

SPIRITS AND MEDICINE MEN

Spirits were everywhere on the Great Plains. They lived in the sky, the earth, and the rivers. Each animal had its own spirit, with a power for good or evil. The Indians believed it was important to live in harmony with all these spirits, as if they were members of their tribe. For this reason, prayers, offerings, and religious ceremonies were very important.

SPIRIT RATTLE

This rattle was shaken by a medicine man, as he called on the spirits for help. Drums, rattles, pipes, and other musical instruments could also be used to scare away evil spirits, or to create a mood of religious excitement during dances and other important ceremonies.

◄ Guidance from the spirits

A medicine man falls into a trance, hoping to receive the power to cure a dying man. Before asking for spirit guidance, most medicine men tried remedies based on plants and herbs. Some of these worked, others did not. But that did not really matter. The Indians believed that the Great Spirit decided whether the patient would recover.

► Medicine man

A painting by Karl Bodmer, showing a medicine man from the Mandan tribe. He is dressed in elaborate clothes, including a bear claw necklace and embroidered leggings. His buffalo skin cloak is painted with special designs. In his hand, he carries a long peace pipe, decorated with hair and feathers.

Spirits helped the Indians to find food and shelter. They could bring success in battle, or protect travelers on dangerous journeys. Offending them brought bad luck, and could cause crop failure, injuries, or sickness. So Indians made offerings of their best dogs and horses or their most beautiful possessions, to show their thanks and keep the spirits happy.

Medicine men

Offerings, prayers, and dances could link people with the powerful spirit world. *Medicine men* (also called healers or shamans) claimed that they spoke with the spirits and received help and guidance from them. They used music, fasting (going without food), and occasionally, herbs to fall into a trance. They left their bodies behind and moved in the shadowy land of the spirits. While they were in trances the medicine men spoke strange words, which were carefully listened to and followed as good advice. When people fell ill, medicine men asked the spirits to send down the power to make them well. Medicine men also prayed and chanted, asking the spirits to protect the tribe's warriors, or to send rain during droughts.

MEDICINE BUNDLES

These were collections of beads, bones, stones, and feathers, carefully wrapped in skin or cloth. Each object had a special meaning. It reminded people of ancient myths and legends, and had special powers. Medicine bundles were treasured in families, and were handed down from father to son.

INDIAN CRAFTS

Indian craftworkers, both men and women, were very skillful. Today, we admire the objects they made for their colors, patterns, and designs. But to the Indians, many of the things they made had special meanings. They were a record of their owner's life or achievements, or showed his or her position within the tribe. Some designs had a magic all of their own. Sacred symbols painted on shields, for example, were believed to protect a warrior from enemy arrows and spears.

▲ Painted hide

A pouch made of painted hide, decorated with geometric patterns. Designs like these were often used on parfleches—larger containers, also made of hide— used to store dried meat on long journeys. The patterns on this pouch may symbolize the sun, or stand for "long life" or "the seasons."

▲ The old and the new

A gun case, made of deerskin, decorated with plaited leather and fringes. Even modern weapons, like guns, were decorated using traditional Indian craft skills.

▶ History pictures

Part of a painting on deerskin, showing warriors chasing their prey. Paintings like this were traditionally made by men, to record their family's achievements. In some tribes, specially painted skins were kept, recording important events every year.

Buffalo skins, bones, horns, and hair were the raw materials for many Indian crafts. Hides were fringed and painted, or sewn with feathers, porcupine quills, and beads. Bones and horns were drilled and carved. Indians also wove baskets, carved wooden cradle boards for carrying babies on their backs, and used dried corn husks to make dolls for the children to play with. They made necklaces and earrings from bear and beaver teeth. Painters and dyers made paints from bark, beetles, natural materials, and colored earth. Women in the villages made cooking pots in simple kilns.

Trading goods

Until the arrival of white American traders, the Indians had no shops. They had to make everything they needed themselves. But most tribes were not completely self-sufficient. They traded their own specialized products for objects made in neighboring lands. Indian craft skills continued long after contact with traders, but they were changed in several ways. The traders brought metal. Soon arrows, tomahawks, and spears were fitted with metal blades. Indian blacksmiths were very skilled at recycling scrap metal from broken stoves, twisted gun barrels, and camp-fire kettles.

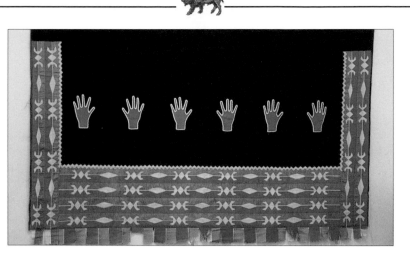

▲ Hands up
Blanket bought from settlers but decorated by women from the Osage tribe with an Indian design of appliquéd (sewn-on) ribbon. These objects reveal the skills of Indian workers, even when using foreign raw materials.

▼ Carefully woven
A rare example of an Indian rush mat, woven by Pawnee women. Mats like this were used to cover the floor inside tepees and earth lodges. Because they are made of fragile materials, they hardly ever survive.

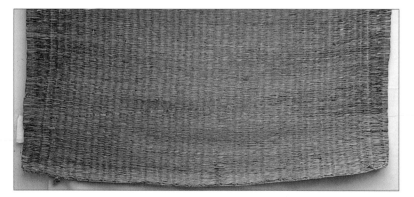

WEAVING WITH QUILLS

Indian women used porcupine quills to decorate clothes, shoes, and headdresses. The quills were colored with dyes made from plants, flattened, then woven or plaited, ready to be sewn or glued onto leather.

▲ Flattening quill with polished bone tool.

▲ Quills were wrapped around hair or across threads.

▲ Quills woven together in a crisscross pattern.

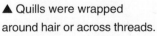
▲ Quills plaited together to form a wide band.

INDIAN CLOTHES

Many of us think we know what the Plains Indians looked like. Sometimes we are right, but all too often our image is based on the Indians we have seen in films, comics, and on television. There, Indians are often shown wearing the wrong sorts of clothes at inappropriate times. Indian clothing was well made, practical, and often very attractive. Like other Indian crafts, it carried a special meaning.

"RED" INDIANS

Two Indian warriors, magnificently dressed in buffalo-skin cloaks. The warrior on the right is wearing face paint. This was partly as disguise, and partly to make him look impressive. Some historians think that the old, disrespectful name Red Indians originated because of the Indians' habit of painting themselves with red earth.

Early travelers to the Plains reported that the Indians were tall, handsome, and proud of their appearance. Sadly, they reported that many women lost their good looks after they were married, because of all the hard work and early childbearing.

Before white settlers arrived on the Plains, Indian men and women wore very little clothing in the hot summer months. Unlike the Christian settlers, they did not see any reason to cover themselves up. Long clothes got in the way and, in any case, Indians admired beautiful bodies. Men wore a loincloth, while women wore an apron or a fringed miniskirt. Children were often naked.

In colder weather, men and women covered up with long, fur-lined cloaks. Women in tribes who lived in the coolest regions of the Plains wore shirts or dresses in summer, while the men wore loose-fitting leggings. All these clothes were made of buffalo skin and decorated with paint, quills, and beads. People went barefoot or wore buffalo-hide moccasins. Both men and women wore splendid jewelery, and some tribes used earth and vegetable dyes to paint their faces. Once they started trading with outsiders, many Plains Indians began wearing ribbons, blankets, and woven cloth.

▲ For hands and feet

Wealthy or important Indians wore fine shoes and gloves like those above. Top: moccasin boots, trimmed with bead embroidery. From the Cree tribe, probably nineteenth century. Center: moccasin shoes, made of deerskin and decorated with beads. Kiowa tribe, nineteenth century. Bottom: gloves made of white deerskin, with fringing and bead decoration. Cree, nineteenth century.

▲ Hidatsa shirt

A man's shirt is made out of soft buckskin. It is decorated with porcupine-quill embroidery and cut fringes. Shirts like this were admired by European travelers to the Plains. They described them as being soft and white as Chinese silk. Womens' shirts were similar in style, and might be trimmed with ermine fur.

Men's shirts could also be decorated with fur, or with scalplocks. These were patches of human skin with long strands of hair attached, cut from an enemy's head.

WINTER WEAR

Indians living on the cold northern Plains made snowshoes like these, to stop themselves from sinking into deep drifts. Rawhide strips were laced over a framework of twigs. Soft skin thongs held the snowshoes in place.

CROWNING GLORIES

Some men did not cut their hair. Travelers described Crow chiefs with hair trailing on the ground, "black and shiny like a raven's wing." Men plucked their beards or shaved with shells.

Women's hairstyles were simpler than men's; often, their hair was worn long and loose. Many women decorated the center part with red paint.

▲ Crow warrior with raised, stiffened fringe, long hair, and hair ornaments.

▲ Shaved head and *roach* (spiked) hairstyle, made of deer hair and turkey feathers

▲ Long, smooth, oiled hair, and plaits decorated with otter fur.

killed an enemy

struck wounded enemy

third coup achieved

fourth coup achieved

fifth coup achieved

red spot for killing enemy

notch for cutting
enemy's throat

▼ ...a warrior brave
When war was declared, all the warriors who were willing to fight smoked a ceremonial pipe, put on their best clothes and weapons, and joined in a war dance, promising to fight bravely and not run away. Indian warriors were volunteers. They despised American government soldiers, who fought for pay.

learned to trust in the Great Spirit, who stayed with the young man through all his suffering.

Pride and honor

Indian warriors were also very proud. Some insults were unforgivable, and led to furious fights. The artist George Catlin recalled how he once made a portrait of Maho Tcheega (Little Bear), a famous Mandan warrior. It showed him in a noble pose. Everyone in the tribe admired the painting, except one troublemaker, who said that since it only showed one side of Maho Tcheega's face, he could only be half a man. This was a great insult. In the fight that followed, Maho Tcheega was killed.

Dangerous raids

Native American tribes had always quarreled, competing for the most fertile fields or the best

▼ Picturesque and thrilling
This nineteenth century picture of a Blackfoot warrior riding his war pony shows how some European travelers saw the Plains Indians. In 1831, Catlin described Blackfoot warriors as "picturesque (attractive) and thrilling." He was also very impressed by their fighting skills.

▼ Tough training

Indian boys trained hard. They ran races, wrestled, practiced riding, and learned how to shoot arrows and throw spears. In many tribes, a young man was mocked if he became too fat, or if he preferred to spend his time around the camp, talking to the women. He could never become...

AIMING TO KILL

Before settlers brought guns, Indians had many different types of bows and arrows. Plains Indian bows were made of wood (usually ash), bone, or horn, with a layer of buffalo sinew along the outside, to make them strong and flexible. The sinew was soaked in water and softened (women chewed it). Then it was fixed to the bow using glue made from turtle shell. Indian bows were short, three feet long (1 m), but very powerful.

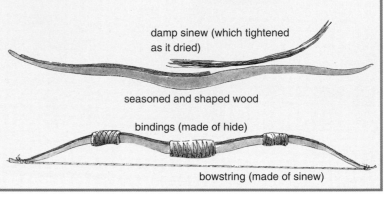

damp sinew (which tightened as it dried)

seasoned and shaped wood

bindings (made of hide)

bowstring (made of sinew)

hunting grounds. Once horses arrived on the Plains, they provided a new reason for war. Tribes without horses, or who wanted more, set out on raids. They traveled long distances, walking 25 miles (40 km) a day and living on dried meat or whatever they could catch. At night, they attacked an enemy camp, rounded up the horses, and rode off. These raids were very dangerous. More men were killed stealing horses than in many wars.

Weapons and war

Traditionally, Plains Indians fought with bows and arrows, tomahawks, clubs, and spears. Arrow heads and spear tips were made of stone, carefully trimmed to a razor-sharp edge. This was hard, skillful work. Stone chips were also used to make tomahawk blades and to add to the heads

▲ Ready for war

An Indian warrior of the Mandan tribe, painted by Bodmer in 1834. He is clutching a metal-bladed tomahawk (or hatchet) and wearing war paint. He is also wearing exploit feathers in his hair—signs that he has killed men in battle, or performed other brave deeds.

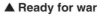

▲ War and peace

A pipe tomahawk, often described as an Indian warrior's most valued weapon. In peacetime, it allowed him to smoke, and was useful for chopping firewood when making camp fires far away from home. In war, it served as a deadly ax, sometimes used in hand-to-hand fighting, and sometimes thrown at an enemy's head.

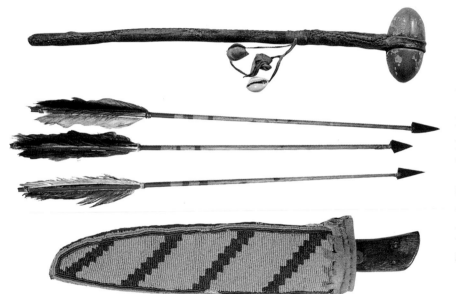

▲ Deadly weapons

Top: Sioux war club, made of wood, stone, and leather.
Center: war arrows, made of cane with metal tips, and decorated with feathers and paint. A warrior could shoot 15 or 20 arrows every minute. Indian bows, made of wood and bone, were small, but powerful.
Bottom: a metal knife, purchased from traders, in a leather case trimmed with beadwork in traditional Indian patterns.

of clubs. Bows were made from buffalo bones or the antlers of deer.

Until European settlers arrived, the Plains Indians did not know how to work iron. They soon learned, and metal began to replace stone as the cutting edge of many weapons. White traders also sold large numbers of sharp metal knives to Indian braves. These replaced their bone tools.

Knives were important, but Indian warfare was changed even more by other European imports—gunpowder and guns. Like horses, guns gave tribes who had them a great advantage over their enemies. They could kill more buffalo, faster.

New wars

During the nineteenth century, the Plains Indians' reasons for fighting changed. Immigrants were flocking to America from many parts of Europe. The whites pushed westward and were soon settling all over Indian land. Miners also wanted to dig gold from Indian territory. Before long, the Plains Indians were having to fight for their land and lives.

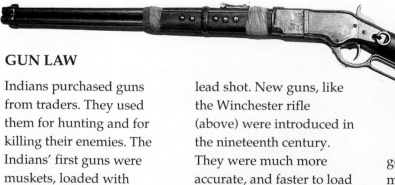

GUN LAW

Indians purchased guns from traders. They used them for hunting and for killing their enemies. The Indians' first guns were muskets, loaded with gunpowder, and firing lead shot. New guns, like the Winchester rifle (above) were introduced in the nineteenth century. They were much more accurate, and faster to load and fire. Before the Indians got them, their fighting men could not hope to win against U.S. army troops.

▼ New people, new homes

The Indians had been made homeless because new settlers arrived. They took over Indian territory, and built farms, houses, churches, and even towns on the empty Great Plains. Most settlers came from Europe, and brought their European life-style with them. Their houses and shops were built to European designs.

They sold imported European goods, drove European horses and carts, and wore European clothing. They introduced European laws, social customs, and religious beliefs.

To many of these settlers, the Indians were almost invisible. They did not understand, or care about, the Indian way of life.

SETTLERS

In 1563, the French explorer Jacques Cartier met Indian tribes living along the banks of the St. Lawrence River, near what is now the U.S. border with Canada. They greeted him peacefully and with kindness. Cartier's reaction was not so friendly. He saw the Indians as animals, and wrote back to the French king that he hoped they would be "easy to tame."

◄ An empty land?

Indian villages were scattered at great distances from one another. Nomadic tribes ranged over hundreds of miles of territory. It was possible to travel for several days without seeing another human being—or even many birds and animals. Even so, the Great Plains were not uninhabited. They were the Indians' home. But by 1900, the Plains Indians were homeless. How had this happened…?

Cartier's reaction to the Native American people he met was typical of many other European settlers who followed him. In 1787, the United States Congress tried to protect the Indians, decreeing that "in their property, rights and liberty, they never shall be…disturbed." But this well-meaning law was usually ignored.

Settlers reach the Plains

By the 1830s, troubles caused by settlers reached the Plains. European diseases killed thousands; only 160 members of the whole Mandan nation survived the smallpox epidemic of 1837–38. Traders encouraged the Indians to stop making traditional goods and tried to get them to depend on food and clothes bought at company stores. Congress created new states, carving up Indian territory and refusing to recognize Indian rights to land.

Even worse, both settlers and the government failed to understand the Indians' way of life. Hunters with guns were allowed to slaughter the great buffalo herds. In three years, from 1872 through 1874, they slaughtered 3,550,000 buffalo; by 1900, only 39 animals survived. They killed deer, beavers, and many other species, until the Indians faced starvation. Migrants were encouraged to set up farms on the open Plains and put up fences to keep the Indians out. New towns and villages sprung up all over the Plains, and religious sites were spoiled.

▲ Buffalo's last home
Palo Duro Canyon. This remote valley became a refuge for the last wild herds of buffalo, as they were shot by settlers, or driven away from their ancient grazing lands. It was also a stronghold for a group of Cheyenne warriors, who were the last Indians to keep on fighting against U.S. government and settler troops.

◄ Wagon train
Groups of settlers, in covered wagons, resting beside the Washita River, Oklahoma, around 1890. Settlers like these were given Indian land by the U.S. government.

SURVIVORS

The Sioux chief Tatanka Yotanka (Sitting Bull) is one of the best-known Indian leaders. He spent almost all of his life fighting for Indian rights. Bitterly, he described what had happened to the Plains Indians people: "You have taken our lands and made us outcasts."

▼ **Politics and war**
A group of Crow chiefs and warriors photographed on a visit to discuss Indian affairs with the U.S. government in Washington D.C. Several Indian leaders made attempts to negotiate peacefully with the settlers and the government, but agreement proved impossible.

Sitting Bull died, shot by a soldier, in 1890. By that time, the traditional life-style of his people had been almost totally destroyed. Plains Indians could no longer live as nomads. They were driven out of their traditional homelands and herded onto reservations, where they had to earn a living in any way they could. Their traditional skills were useless there, and disease, depression, and despair quickly set in.

With astonishing arrogance, missionaries and teachers tried to "civilize" Indian tribes. Traditional ceremonies were banned. Indian children were taken from their parents and sent away to white schools. They were made to cut their hair, given English names, trained in white American ways, and beaten if they spoke their own languages.

▲ **Changing lives**
Quanah Parker, a chief of the Comanche tribe with one of his wives, Tonasa. Here he shows that he has adapted to a European style of life, dressed in their clothes and living in a house. However, he took up arms against the slaughter of the last herds of buffalo on the southern Plains.

RESERVATIONS

This map shows land where the Indians were allowed to live by the U.S. government, at the end of the nineteenth century. Reservation life was grim, but Indians who refused to move were labeled troublemakers, and many were shot as U.S. troops advanced to protect the settlers' lands. As one Sioux warrior protested, "When the white man comes into my country, he leaves a trail of blood behind him."

When they left school, they felt out of place back home with their families. In white society they were only offered dead-end jobs and faced racial hatred.

In search of "Red Power"

In the early twentieth century, determined Indian leaders, helped by a few sympathetic white politicians, struggled to protect their people. Leading Americans often showed appalling prejudice, but Indian protesters continued to compaign for civil rights.

Life is still hard for Indians today. In many parts of the Untied States and Canada, they are the poorest, least healthy, and worst-educated people. Indian leaders have clashed with the government and one another. Tourism and the packaging of Indian culture for entertainment presents another threat. But, so far, the Indian people have survived.

▲ Living traditions
An Indian powwow (tribal meeting) held on the northern Plains in 1985. Indians gathered here, in a modern tepee camp, to remember their ancestors' way of life.

▶ A modern Indian
A Blackfoot dancer, wearing a modern version of traditional clothes, which are decorated with bone and feathers. He wears face paint and a roach headdress.

PLAINS INDIANS TIME CHART

This time chart looks at the lives of the Native American people who lived on and around the Great Plains. For many centuries, they had hunted and farmed here, but their traditional life-style was dramatically changed by the arrival of European settlers.

NATIVE AMERICANS

The Plains Indians were just one of many groups of Native peoples who lived in North America. Each group had evolved a way of life that enabled it to survive in harmony with the harsh environments of America's vast and varied land.

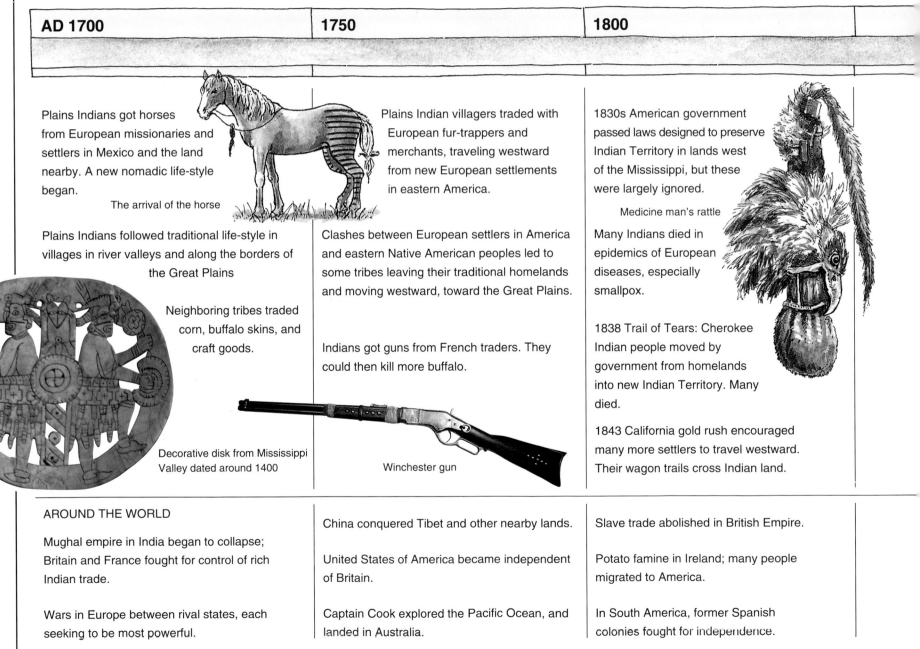

AD 1700	1750	1800

Plains Indians got horses from European missionaries and settlers in Mexico and the land nearby. A new nomadic life-style began.

The arrival of the horse

Plains Indians followed traditional life-style in villages in river valleys and along the borders of the Great Plains

Neighboring tribes traded corn, buffalo skins, and craft goods.

Decorative disk from Mississippi Valley dated around 1400

Plains Indian villagers traded with European fur-trappers and merchants, traveling westward from new European settlements in eastern America.

Clashes between European settlers in America and eastern Native American peoples led to some tribes leaving their traditional homelands and moving westward, toward the Great Plains.

Indians got guns from French traders. They could then kill more buffalo.

Winchester gun

1830s American government passed laws designed to preserve Indian Territory in lands west of the Mississippi, but these were largely ignored.

Medicine man's rattle

Many Indians died in epidemics of European diseases, especially smallpox.

1838 Trail of Tears: Cherokee Indian people moved by government from homelands into new Indian Territory. Many died.

1843 California gold rush encouraged many more settlers to travel westward. Their wagon trails cross Indian land.

AROUND THE WORLD

Mughal empire in India began to collapse; Britain and France fought for control of rich Indian trade.

Wars in Europe between rival states, each seeking to be most powerful.

China conquered Tibet and other nearby lands.

United States of America became independent of Britain.

Captain Cook explored the Pacific Ocean, and landed in Australia.

Slave trade abolished in British Empire.

Potato famine in Ireland; many people migrated to America.

In South America, former Spanish colonies fought for independence.

Inuit (before 5000 BC onward)

Northwest coast (7000 BC–AD 1600)

California and Southwest (2000 BC–AD 1600)

Great Plains Indians (before AD 1 onward)

European settlers (1492 onward)

1850	1900	1950

Many new settlers arrived in Indian Territory. The American government allowed them to take land free, or to purchase it at very low rates, despite earlier government promises about preserving Indian land.

Railways were built across Indian lands, and destroyed buffalo hunting grounds.

The buffalo

1860–1890 Bitter fighting between settlers, U.S. government troops, and Indian people, as Plains Indians struggled to preserve their homeland and their traditional way of life. Indians finally defeated at the Battle of Wounded Knee, 1890.

Indians lost control of almost all their homelands. Between 1861–1900, twelve new American states had been created, many in Indian land. During the same period, American population rose from 31 million to 90 million, largely as a result of new settlers arriving from Europe. Indian population fell.

Indians were forced to live on government-controlled reservations.

Buffalo almost extinct, because of slaughter by settlers.

Open Great Plains divided up into fields and farms.

A few Indian politicians continued to campaign for Indian rights.

Growth of civil rights movement among Black Americans encouraged similar demands from Indian groups.

Increasing awareness in Indian heritage among many Americans and people from other lands. Indian traditional legends and histories were collected, and old craft skills were revived. Tourists visit reservations and watch recreated Indian ceremonies and dances.

Beaded moccasins

Taiping Rebellion against emperor in China. Many people killed.

First oil wells drilled in America.

Russian serfs (peasants) freed.

American Civil War.

The two world wars devastated Europe and parts of the Far East.

Advances in science (especially life sciences and medicine) and technology; powered flight, telephones, films, radio, television, domestic machinery all in use in Western world.

Many African states became independent.

First space flights

Growth of Green movement—leads to new appreciation of Plains Indians' attitude to the environment.

GLOSSARY

(Note: Words in *italics* refer to other entries in the Glossary.)

Ancestors People from whom we are descended—grandparents, great-grandparents, and all past generations of a family.

Bark The outer covering of tree trunks, which acts rather like a skin. Some varieties of trees have bark that can be peeled off in large sheets, about one-fifth on an inch (5 mm) thick. Plains Indians used these sheets as a covering for houses and temporary shelters.

Braves Successful and respected Plains Indian *warriors*.

Brushwood Thick, bushy twigs.

Ceremony A special occasion, with prayers, songs, dances, and feasting. Plains Indian people held ceremonies for several different reasons—for example, to give thanks to the Great Spirit or to ask for the Spirit's help; to celebrate a good harvest or to encourage the crops to grow; to mark the end of childhood and the beginning of adult life.

Chief The leader of an Indian tribe, clan, or band.

Citizenship Belonging to a nation. In most countries, being a citizen guarantees certain rights, such as the right to vote, the right to live there permanently, and the right to be protected by the law.

Crops Plants grown for food. The Plains Indians' main crop was *maize*.

Dead-end job A job with no prospects of improvement—for example, no chance of taking on more responsibility or earning a higher wage.

Drought A time when rain does not fall, and water supplies run short.

Environment Surroundings—including the landscape, the weather, and the local plants and animals.

Ermine A small animal, sometimes known as a stoat, which has beautiful fur that turns white in winter, all except for the black tip of its tail. The Plains Indians hunted and killed ermine and used their fur to decorate dresses and shirts.

Herbs Plants that can be eaten. Often used to describe plants with a strong taste and smell, and are used to flavor other foods.

Hit-and-run A way of fighting, where soldiers attack their enemies and then run (or ride) away, rather than staying in one place and fighting hand-to-hand. Today, hit-and-run is also used to describe motorists who do not stop after an accident where someone has been hit by a passing car.

Hospitality Welcoming and caring for visitors.

Ice Age A time (before 10,000 BC) when the Earth's climate changed, and the whole world became much colder. Large ice caps spread from the Arctic and Antarctic, and covered vast areas of land. Because so much water was frozen in these ice caps, the sea level fell, and parts of today's ocean floor became dry land. This was what happened to the land between present-day Alaska and Siberia. A land bridge appeared, and people traveled across it from Asia to settle in North and South America.

Inhabitants The people who live in a particular place.

Kiln A special sort of oven— which can get very hot—where pottery is baked or fired. After firing, pots become stronger and, usually, better able to hold water.

Lacrosse A game rather like hockey, played by certain Indian tribes. Instead of using a stick to hit the ball along the ground, players scooped it up and threw it, using a long-handled net.

Legend An ancient story. Some legends contained scraps of half-remembered fact, passed down over the centuries. Others told stories that had been invented. But whether or not they were true, legends were important in Plains Indian society, because they described ideas and beliefs which the Indians valued highly, and which helped them run their lives.

Loincloth Clothing, worn by men. Some loincloths were just small aprons of cloth, worn front and back, hanging from a string tied around the waist. Others were more elaborate; a long strip of cloth was wrapped around the body, somewhat like a baby's diaper. The resulting garment looked a bit like a pair of shorts.

Maize A tall plant that yields seed heads (called cobs) of juicy kernels. They can be eaten fresh, or dried and then ground to make flour. Maize is also known as corn, sweet corn, or, when fresh, corn on the cob. Popcorn is made from specially treated dried maize.

Migration Moving from one place to another to live.

Minerals Substances, like iron or silicia, that occur naturally in the *environment*. Minerals often combine together to make rocks and gemstones.

Missionary A person who travels to another land to teach people about a new religion.

Moccasin Shoes or boots made and worn by Plains Indians people. Moccasins were sewn by women, and were made of soft, strong leather.

Native Someone who lives in a particular land, and whose *ancestors* have lived there for a long time before.

Noble Savage The belief that people living in non-European countries, and whose way of life was simple, were somehow better and wiser than people living in towns because they lived close to nature.

Pemmican A concentrated food made from dried meat, pounded fine, and mixed with melted fat.

Porcupine An animal (about the size of a very large cat) that lived on the Great Plains. Porcupines were covered in long, sharp spines. Plains Indians killed porcupines and used their quills to decorate their clothing.

Prairie Open grassland.

Prehistoric From the time before history, that is, before people began to keep records (in words or pictures) of past events.

Prey A bird, animal (or person) that is hunted and caught.

Reservation Area of land set aside for Indians to live in by the U.S. government at the end of the nineteenth century.

Ritual Special words and actions used at a religious (or any other) *ceremony*.

Rocky Mountains A range of high mountains running from north to south along the western coast of Canada and the United States.

Rushes Plants, rather like thick, strong grass, that grow in water. When cut and dried, they can be woven to make baskets and mats.

Scalp The skin covering a person's head, where the hair grows. Indian *warriors* tried to capture the scalps of their enemies. This did not always involve killing them. If only a patch of skin and hair were removed, the scalped man might recover.

Settlers People coming to live in a new land. In the nineteenth century, millions of settlers arrived in America, hoping to make a new life for themselves. They did not consider the needs or the rights of the Plains Indian people, on whose land they came to settle.

Smallpox A very dangerous disease. Sufferers are covered in spots and have a high fever. Very often, they die. Smallpox was brought to America by European travelers and traders. Because it was a new disease, it proved particularly dangerous for Indian people.

Snowshoes Little platforms (looking rather like tennis racquets) that could be strapped to the feet. They helped Indians walk in deep snow, by spreading a person's weight over a wider area than the sole of his or her foot. This meant that walkers did not sink so far into the snow.

Stockade A stronge fence, usually made of wood.

Squash A plant related to pumpkins and gourds.

Territory The limited amount of land inhabited by groups of people.

Tradition Habits and beliefs that have been used for a long time, and which are respected and admired.

Vitamins Substances found in foods that are essential for good health. For example, vitamin C, which is found in many fruits, helps wounds to heal and fights infections. Without it, people become very ill and can even die.

Warrior A man trained as a fighter.

Word-of-mouth A message, *tradition*, or belief that is passed on only by being spoken and remembered, not by being written down.

INDEX

(Page numbers in *italics* refer to illustrations and captions.)